The Tinkle Fairy's
guide to where to powder your nose

Written by:
Mark D. Donnelly, PhD.

RPSS–Rock Paper Safety Scissors Publishing
Buffalo, New York

Copyright © 2025 by Dr. Mark D. Donnelly

Text and design by Mark D. Donnelly, Ph.D.
AI images generated by Craiyon.com

All rights reserved. No part of this publication may be reproduced, distributed, or transmitted in any form or by any means, including photocopying, recording, or other electronic or mechanical methods, without the prior written permission of the publisher, except in the case of brief quotations embodied in critical reviews and certain other noncommercial uses permitted by copyright law. For permission requests, write to the publisher at the address below.

RPSS - Rock Paper [Safety] Scissors Publishing
429 Englewood Avenue • Buffalo, New York 14223

www.rpsspublishing.com

The Tinkle Fairy's Guide to Where to Powder Your Nose
Perfect Bound - ISBN:978-1-956688-46-7

10 9 8 7 6 5 4 3 2 1

Printed in the United States of America

Everything you'll ever need to know about the history, euphemisms, and etymology of excrement disposal, plus a shit-ton* more.

*An ass load is the amount of dead weight a healthy adult mule can safely carry which is 20% of it's body weight.
An average mule weighs around 850 lbs
Back of the napkin math is (850*20%)*24 = 4080 lbs
A shit ton is equivalent to 24 ass loads

Butt load" is a real measurement used originally by pirates as two hogheads or half a ton
1 butt load = 126 gallons = 2 hogsheads
1 shit ton = 2 buttloads or 4 hogsheads
1 shit ton = 252 gallons = 953 liters
A metric shit ton = 1000 liters, so it's slightly larger than the US shit ton.

CONTENTS

7
I May Be A Little While

8
The Wonderful World of Poop

22
Answering The Call of Nature

42
Sitting Pretty

90
Making a Clean Sweep

104
False Alarms

123
Who Wrote This Crap

Foreword

I may be a while.

While sitting in the small reading room contemplating some of the world's most unsolvable problems, remember to deliver on your primary objective.

Shit happens. *(Source: Bumper sticker on back of pickup truck.)*

Poop is the great equalizer. All food, every bite and regardless of cost, from a bowl of Fruit Loops to a steak and lobster dinner, turns to poop. No exceptions.

With only one exception, everyone on earth, rich and poor alike poop*. The need to urinate and defecate is one of the things that ties all humans together. From the cradle to the grave, starting with diapers from birth and to adult diapers (from well, it depends), with toilets in between, our lives are a continuum of places to discharge human waste.

Over a lifetime, you will produce roughly 25,000 pounds of poop, which is about 360 pounds per year. You will also create enough urine to fill a backyard swimming pool.

Always be sure to wash your hands.

In the official biography of Kim Jong-il, the author writes that the North Korean leaders were too perfect to need to urinate or defecate. "...Kim Il-sung and Kim Jong-il were perfect beings, untarnished by base human function.

Source: Hindustan Times, New Delhi

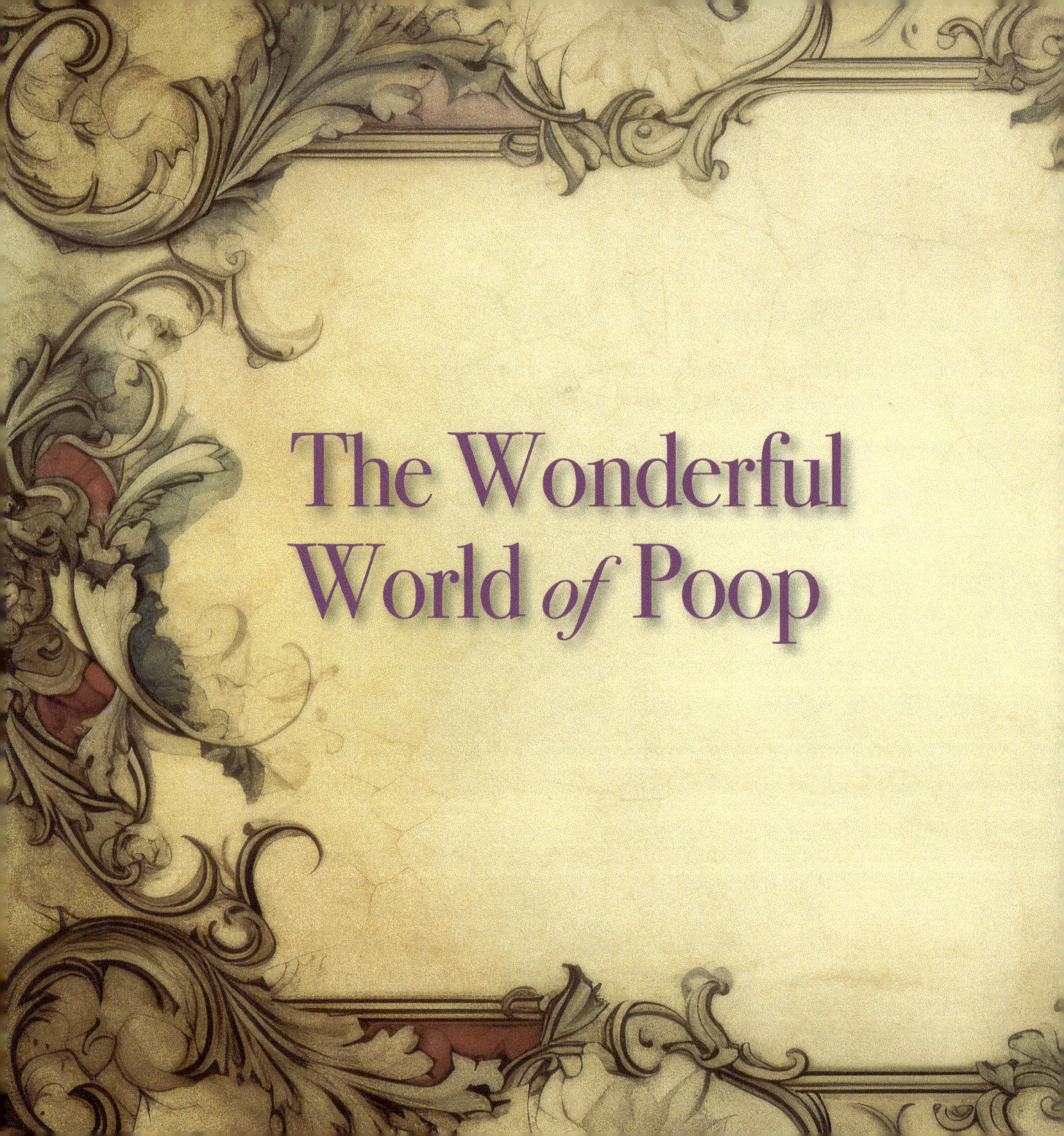

The Wonderful World *of* Poop

The need to expel human waste has spawned a vast array of euphemisms. Here is a selection that is no way comprehensive. Some are more explicit than others so don't read on if you're easily offended.

I suppose that's why we have euphemisms in the first place.

"You're so full of shit, if you ever had an enema you'd evaporate into thin air."

— Catherine Doyle, Mafiosa

"I've been accused of vulgarity. I say that's bullshit."

— Mel Brooks

"I was talking to my friend from New York yesterday, and I used the expression, 'You can't polish a turd'. He looked at me, disgusted, and said, 'No, you can't, but you can roll it in glitter'. He's a lovely guy but I wouldn't want to go to a craft fair with him.

– Steve Williams

Shit Happens

Humans have a rocky relationship with randomness. On the one hand, we declare that "shit happens"--an acknowledgment that bad things sometimes occur for no particular reason. But more often than not, our minds resist randomness, searching for meaning even where none exists.

It's a comforting fact that shit really does happen. Everyone poops. The need to urinate and defecate is one of the things that ties all humans together. While we might not often talk about it, maybe we ought to. Some of this shit is deadly serious.

Globally, humans and livestock animals collectively produce an estimated 8.6 trillion pounds) of feces annually, with human feces comprising 21% of that total. A child is changed an average of 10,000 times before he learns to use the toilet by himself.

Each year, over 200 million tons (181 million metric tons) of human waste goes untreated, with more than 90 percent of sewage in the developing world released directly into oceans, lakes and rivers. According to WHO, around the world, 2.3 billion people do not have basic sanitation facilities.

Clean toilets and water aren't just important for the reasons you might think. In fact, access to sanitation facilities plays a vital role in reducing preventable deaths around the world. About 842,000 people die every year due to inadequate water, sanitation, and hygiene in low and middle income countries.

One of the main causes of death related to sanitation is diarrhea. It is estimated that 801,000 children under the age of 5 die from diarrhea. That translates to about 2,200 children deaths every day. Open defecation plays a large role in those deaths of children. Almost 892 million people still practice open defecation.

Access to toilets doesn't just affect children and incite illness, it also puts women and girls at risk, as finding hidden places to defecate increases their chance of rape and attack. It also makes managing menstruation difficult and it perpetuates a cycle of poverty.

Rate Your Poop

The Bristol stool scale is a medical aid designed to classify the form of human feces into seven categories.

The seven types of stool are:

Type 1: Marbles - Hard and separate little lumps (hard to pass). These little pellets typically mean you're constipated. It shouldn't happen frequently.

Type 2: Caterpillar -Log-shaped but lumpy. Here we have another sign of constipation that, again, shouldn't happen frequently.

Type 3: Hot dog - Log-shaped with some cracks on the surface.
This is the gold standard of poop, somewhat soft and easy to pass.

Type 4: Snake - Smooth and snake-like.
Doctors also consider this a normal poop that should happen every 1–3 days.

Type 5: Amoebas -Small, like the first ones, but soft and easy to pass; the blobs also have clear-cut edges.
This type of poop means you're lacking fiber and should find ways to add some to your diet through cereal or vegetables.

Type 6: Soft serve - Fluffy and mushy with ragged edges.
This too-soft consistency could be a sign of mild diarrhea. Try drinking more water and electrolyte-infused beverages to help improve this.

Type 7: Jackson Pollock - Completely watery with no solid pieces.
In other words, you've got the runs or diarrhea. This means your stool moved through your bowels very quickly and didn't form into a healthy poop.

The smell is subjective but can be rated on the 1 through 10 Donnelly Olfactory Scale, with 1 being "Not Flowers" and 10 being Love Canal Biohazard.

Why Do Turds Float?

Ever noticed how some of your number twos float while others sink without a trace? It turns out, this strange bathroom mystery might actually reveal a lot about the health of your gut bacteria.

About 10 to 15 per cent of people consistently fart out a lump that float in toilet water – so-called "floaters", while the rest typically produce stink brownies that sink to the bottom, or "sinkers".

For years, people assumed fat made stools buoyant, but studies show it's actually gas—produced by microbes during digestion. Research led by Dr. Kannan at the Mayo Clinic revealed that germ-free mice had sinking poop, while those given gut bacteria developed floaters.

The key difference? Microbes like Bacteroides ovatus, which ferment food and release gas, making stools lighter. The more gas-producing bacteria you have, the more likely your poop is to float.

Though the studies were on mice, Kannan suspects similar patterns in humans—especially after antibiotics disrupt gut bacteria. While poop science isn't glamorous, it could reveal important clues about gut health and digestion.

In short: a floating deuce might just be your gut microbes doing their gassy thing.

Never kick a fresh turd on a hot day.
– Harry S. Truman

No Shit

Fart jokes are universally funny, and turd jokes are freaking hysterical, but constipation is no joke. The proverbial 'constipated face' is not funny anymore when you're on the throne to get busy and your butt says not today, no matter how hard you try.

Many people don't realize that making healthier food and lifestyle choices can reduce their risk of constipation. The main causes of constipation are typically poor diet and lifestyle habits, and adjusting these can help ease and prevent future discomfort.

Constipation is a common digestive issue characterized by infrequent bowel movements (fewer than three per week), difficulty passing stools, or the feeling of incomplete bowel emptying. Symptoms can include hard stools, bloating, and discomfort. While constipation can resolve on its own, chronic cases may need dietary or lifestyle changes. If symptoms persist, consult a doctor.

Constipation can result from various factors, but poor diet, especially low fiber intake, is a common cause. Other factors include Ignoring the urge to go, medications, insufficient fluids, sedentary lifestyle, Diabetes, IBS, anxiety, or depression.

Focusing on high-fiber, low-fat foods can relieve constipation and support regular bowel movements. Fiber can be soluble, which softens stools, or insoluble, which helps food pass through the gut. Both types help with digestion. Soluble fiber-rich foods include apples, oats, beans, and bananas. Insoluble fiber-rich foods include leafy greens, popcorn, dried fruit, and whole grains.

Certain foods, you know, all the good stuff, can worsen constipation. Limit or avoid dairy, processed foods, fried foods, refined sugars, white bread, and red meat.

This, too, shall pass.

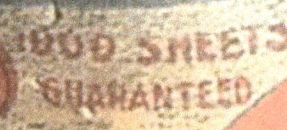

Busting a Grumpy

If you're still using the boring words "Poop" or "No. 2" you should consider upgrading. Here are a bunch of phrases that help keep plumber's employed:

- Dropping a deuce
- Cuttin' rope
- An offering to the porcelain throne
- Pushing a mess
- Building a log cabin
- 3d Printing a Snickers
- Unload some timber
- Make like Snoop and 'Drop it like it's hot'
- Need to void
- Make a deposit in the porcelain bank
- Use the big, white telephone
- Unloose the caboose
- Play dough factory
- Log rolling
- Turd
- Baking a loaf
- Baking brownies
- Catching up on some reading
- Communing with nature
- Crowning
- Decorating the Oval Office
- Delivering a load
- Dirty bombing
- Dropping plunkies
- Dropping a bomb/brick
- Dropping anchor
- Fart out a lump
- Greeting Mr. Hankey
- Growing a monkey tail
- Gotta go
- Gotta sling mud from the back bucket
- Gotta go, I'm touching cloth
- Having the squirts
- Heaving a Havana
- Killing the cobra
- Launching the torpedoes
- Laying cable
- Laying pipe
- Leaving a floater
- Letting loose
- Logging out
- Making fudge
- Making room for dessert
- Making sausage
- Making stinky
- Needing some alone time
- Opening the gates
- Pinching a loaf
- Releasing the Kraken
- Road apples
- Rolling a nut log
- Shooting the Hershey squirts
- Sinking the Bismarck
- Skid mark
- Squeezing one out
- Stocking the pond
- Taking a load off your mind
- Taking a dump
- Taking it to the hoop
- Turtlehead
- Pause for the cause
- Pop a squat

POOZEUM

#1 FOR FOSSILIZED #2 | **WORLD'S LARGEST COLLECTION** | **FREE MUSEUM** | **DINOSAUR GIFT SHOP** | **WORLD'S LARGEST COPROLITE**

Turd Museum

The Poozeum Museum in Arizona houses over 7,000 specimens of coprolites (fossilized dinosaur dookie) from creatures big and small. The collection includes everything from tiny termite droppings to a massive 20-pound duece! With display cases filled with fascinating fossilized feces, the museum holds the Guinness World Record for having the most extensive collection of coprolites.

Described as being #1 for #2, Arizona's fossilized poo museum is free for all to view. The Poozeum is right on Route 66, situated in the charming town of Williams, also known for its Wild West shows, wildlife attractions, and as the gateway to the Grand Canyon National Park.

Poozeum offers a unique way to learn about the prehistoric world. Through coprolites, visitors gain insights into ancient diets and ecosystems. It's a chance to see a rare side of paleontology and understand how something as simple as poop can tell us so much about the past.

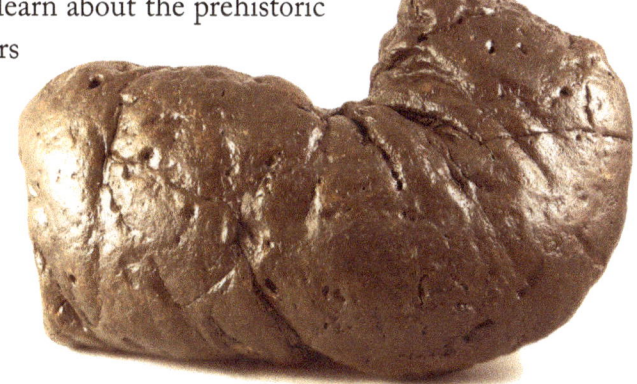

Discovered in South Carolina, this legendary fossilized feces specimen is named "Precious." It is one of the largest true-to-form pieces of fossilized poop in the world. The specimen would be hard to flush and impossible to plunge at 4.5 pounds and over 10" inches long if it wasn't bent.

By Poozeum - Own work, CC BY-SA 4.0,

Answering The Call of Nature

The urge to "go" combined with the proper euphemisms for gracefully excusing yourself is a culturally inspired art form that's been practiced throughout history.

"Peeing in the snow is how little boy's learn cursive."
— Dr. Maddog

"Sometimes the beauty is easy. Sometimes you don't have to try at all. Sometimes you can hear the wind blow in a handshake. Sometimes there's poetry written right on the bathroom wall.
— Ani DiFranco

Powder your nose

Powdering your nose is an early 20th-century euphemism, which is now rather dated. It's is a phrase is a polite expression used to excuse oneself when going to the bathroom, typically used by women.

The term powder room has been used since the 1940s to refer to a ladies' toilet in a hotel, restaurant, or similar public building.

"I'm just going to powder my nose and I'll be with you in a minute."

Powdering your nose also has a more notorious modern meaning, but that requires a whole new book.

Take a Leak/Pee

When someone excuses themselves to "take a leak," I've always wondered why they wouldn't prefer to leave one instead.

To "leak," meaning to "make water" was first a verb.

> *Why, they will allow us ne'er a jordan, and then we leak in your chimney; and your chamber-lie breeds fleas like a loach.*
> —Shakespeare, Henry IV: Part 1

And pee/piss, as a verb, goes back to Middle English.

> *An hound, whan he comth by the roser or by othere beautees, thogh he may nat pisse, yet wole he heue vp his leg and make a contenaunce to pisse.*
> —Chaucer, the Parson's Tale

By the 20th century, both words could also serve as nouns, denoting the action of leaking or pissing, according to the Oxford English Dictionary. At the same time, they acquired a periphrastic use in the phrase to take a leak:

> *"There were puddles of sludge from the mud of the road, the waste water of the saloon, and any number of passing drunkards who thought to stop and take a piss on their way through."*
> — Heartless, 1934

> *"Pull over. I've got to take a leak."*
> —The Godfather (1972)

> *"When people try to rain on your parade,...pee on theirs"*
> —Josh Stern, And That's Why I'm Single

Pay a visit to Mrs. Jones

In Victorian times when you needed to relieve yourself, you would explain that it was necessary to visit Mrs. Jones. Jones isn't a particularly unusual surname so I do wonder how Mrs. Jones felt about this phrase.

More modern excuses range from:
"I need to freshen up"
"Taking in the view"
"Going to the library"
"Doing some research"
"Gotta go check out a book"
"Powder my nose"
"Use the facilities"
"See a man about a horse"

"Pee" is an informal but common word that means "to urinate". It's one of the least offensive slang words for bodily functions.

Synonyms for peeing:
Wee
Tinkle
Piddle
Spend a penny
Pass water
Wee-wee
Micturate
Take a whizz

Taking the Browns to the Super Bowl

The quote "I gotta take the Browns to the Super Bowl" is from the 2009 movie Zombieland. In the movie, Columbus says this line:

Columbus: Hey, this may be a bad time, but I gotta take the Browns to the Super Bowl.

The Cleveland Browns are one of four NFL teams that have never played in the Super Bowl. The other three teams are the Detroit Lions, Houston Texans, and Jacksonville Jaguars. The Browns have won four NFL championships, but all of these were before the Super Bowl was introduced.

An alternative to taking the browns to church and filling up the pews.
I was taking the browns to the Superbowl when two got out before reaching the stadium.

–Ivan Wakinov December 25, 2017

I'm going to see a man about a horse

It means to politely excuse yourself from a situation to go to the restroom or buy a drink. It originated from men disappearing to go bet on horse or dog races. See a man about a dog means the same thing.

The earliest confirmed publication of this explanation is the 1866 Dion Boucicault play *"Flying Scud"* in which a character knowingly breezes past a difficult situation saying, "Excuse me Mr. Quail, I can't stop; I've got to see a man about a dog." In a listing for a 1939 revival on the NBC Radio program America's Lost Plays, Time magazine observed that the phrase is the play's "claim to fame".

During Prohibition in the United States, the phrase see a man about a horse was most commonly used in relation to the consumption or purchase of alcoholic beverages.

The origins date back to the days of the "Not-Quite-So-Wild-Yet-Still-Wild Enough Old West". When at the local drinking establishment the horse trough was closer to the entrance of the building than the outhouses which were generally situated out back. And thus a slang term was born. And of course most people had enough common decency to only use the trough for number one.

I've Been Visited by the Tinkle Fairy

A tinkle fairy is presumably an imaginary being that monitors every moment you urinate, it is mostly known for its limitations, such as 'the amount of times you can shake'. It was made popular from the show Family Guy.

Adam West: *shakes twice*

Tinkle Fairy: Two shakes, that's it...Move along!

Adam West: Oh, why thank you, Tinkle Fairy!

If you can't remember your last uninterrupted night's sleep, it's because the "Tinkle Fairy" has chosen to work the night shift.

Spend a Penny

This British expression is a much more polite way to say you need to use the "loo". It refers to the former use of coin operated locks on public toilets. The phrase was used mostly by women because men's urinals were free of charge.

These locks were introduced at the public toilets outside the Royal Exchange in London in the 1850s but the phrase wasn't recorded until 1945 in H. Spencer Lewis's *"A Thousand Years of Yesterdays: A Strange Story of Mystic Revelations"*.

We need to be glad that this is no longer a thing, but it reminds us that women have been discouraged in ways big and small from being active and independent out in the world, including having to pay up to pee while their male counterparts did it for free! The toilets were for men only for almost 40 years.

The first public underground toilets in the world were located outside the Royal Exchange in London in 1854. The toilets were operated by the City of London and are still in use today featuring their iconic cast iron décor.

"There are few moments of clarity more profound than those that follow the emptying of an overcharged bladder. The world slows down, the focus sharpens, the brain comes back on line. Huge nebulous difficulties prove on close calm examination to be merely cloud giants."

– Tom Holt

You Don't Know Jack Shit

In Ireland 'the jacks' – has long been used to describe the common, everyday toilet. While Thomas Crapper is commonly credited for inventing the first flushing toilet in the late 1800s, the first ever multi-cubicle toilet is traced back to 1806 to Jack Power, an Irish inventor from Thurles, County Tipperary.

Power, a father of 38 children, was the first person in the world to develop a separate cubicle for dropping plunkies in.

Due to the sheer size of his family, Jack had to create something to cater for their simultaneous bowel movements, so he built a large outhouse with five separate toilets. Following its success at home, Jack went on to manufacture cubicles for businesses and soon became very rich from the proceeds.

In 1811, Jack Power was named one of Ireland's richest businessmen, but the pressure of fame and fortune soon took its toll.

Jack originally patented his multiple toilet system and insisted on calling it a 'MultiPoo™', but the people of Ireland preferred 'Jacks' instead – a term earlier coined by his children. This infuriated Jack as he never liked his name associated with going to the toilet. The more he insisted, the more people called the cubicle system 'the Jacks'; this even passed on to single-cell toilets. People on the street would taunt Jack and call him names like 'Jack Shit', which he hated.

Jack would later change his name to Armitage Shank and moved to the UK with his family. There he began inventing new toilet systems, like urinals, and became the world's leading manufacturer in toilet systems, which is still in operation. Following Jack's sudden departure from his home country, another common phrase was also coined by people that knew him, simply put: 'You don't know Jack Shit'.

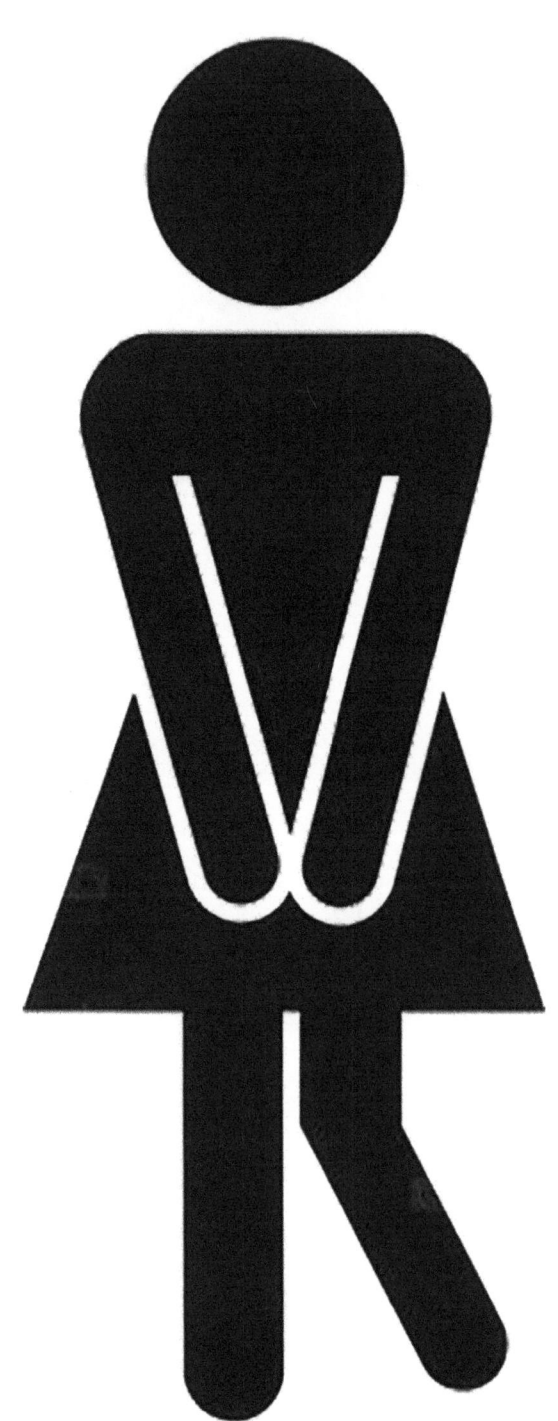

Potty Dance

I grew up with six brothers.
That's how I learned to dance – waiting for the bathroom.
          -Bob Hope

This dance, a combination of subtle and obvious movements, aims to resist the body's natural urges and avoid an embarrassing mishap typically by crossing one's legs, hopping, twitching, or holding one's crotch.

> Step to the left, now step to the right.
> Put your knees together and squeeze 'em tight!
> Keep your arms moving side to side!
> Try to hold it in 'till it's time to ride!
>
> Knock knock, let me in!
> Knock knock, let me in, I gotta go (uh)!
> Knock knock, let me in!
> Knock knock, let me in, I gotta go!
>
> Keep moving now! Don't you stop!
> Hold it in 'till it's time to drop!
> 'Lemme in before I pop!'
> Too late, gotta grab a mop.
>
> Knock knock, let me in!
> Knock knock, let me in, I gotta go (uh)!
> Knock knock, let me in!
> Knock knock, let me in, **I GOTTA GO!**
>   — *Teen Titans Go!, "The Pee Pee Dance"*

This chapter examines the history of toilets, the inventors who transformed sanitation, and how the humble toilet has become a fundamental aspect of modern life.

> *"My name is only an anagram of toilets."*
> -T. S. Eliot

> *"Toilets are more than a graveyard for dead goldfish."*
> - Non Compos Mentis Mongrel, PhD.

Used Food Receptacles

Throughout much of history, humans commonly practiced open defecation or used latrines and outhouses in rural areas. In urban settings, people relied on chamber pots, which were often emptied into streets or drains.

The Bronze Age Indus Valley civilization that flourished in the northwestern regions of South Asia had advanced sanitation systems, including private flush toilets. The ancient Greeks and Romans used public toilets and, in some cases, had indoor plumbing connected to basic sewer systems.

During medieval times, the latrines of monasteries, known as reredorters, were sometimes linked to intricate water systems that effectively disposed of waste without contaminating the community's drinking, cooking, or washing water.

In the early modern period, "night soil" from municipal outhouses became a significant source of nitrates for gunpowder production. The 19th century brought improvements to outhouses, including designs such as the privy midden and the pail closet. Indoor toilets were initially a luxury reserved for the wealthy and only gradually became common among the lower classes.

In the early 20th century, some English homes featured an upstairs toilet for the owners and an outhouse for their servants. Some homes even had toilets built into the house but accessible only from the outside. Following World War I, all new housing in London and its suburbs included indoor toilets. Bathrooms became standard in homes later than toilets, appearing in working-class houses around the same time.

Used Food Receptacles (cont.)

Due to plumbing considerations, flush toilets were usually located in or near bathrooms. Originally, both bathrooms and toilets were often situated above the kitchen for convenience.

In upper-class homes, early modern lavatories operated as washrooms, with sinks typically placed near bedrooms. In contrast, lower-class homes often had only collapsible tubs for bathing. In Britain, there was a long-standing prejudice against placing toilets within bathrooms. When toilets were finally integrated into bathrooms, it was primarily for cost-saving reasons.

Today, American and many European homes typically combine toilets and bathrooms. However, separate toilets remain common in British homes and can still be a builder's option even where having the toilet in the bathroom is the norm. In countries like France and Japan, separate toilets are standard, often for reasons of hygiene and privacy. In modern homes outside of France, if toilets are separate, they usually include a sink.

In Japan, some toilet designs feature a built-in sink that uses waste water for subsequent flushes, allowing users to clean themselves immediately after use. Japanese toilets often provide specific slippers for use inside the toilet, distinct from those worn in the rest of the house.

Roman toilets were communal rows of holes carved into cold, Italian marble slabs. A Roman user and a half dozen friends would sit down together to take a dump. Upon finishing, instead of reaching for a roll of toilet paper, an ancient Roman would often grab an abrasive ceramic disc called pessoi or a tersorium, a "toilet brush for your butt" made from a sponge attached to the end of a stick. They then left it for the next person to use. Now that's true friendship.

MARRIAGE.
This Pot it is A Present Sent,
Some mirth to make is only Meant,
We hope the same you'll not Refuse,
But keep it safe and oft it Use,
When in it you want to P'ss
Remember them who sent you

Thunder Mug

A chamber pot is a portable toilet designed for overnight use in the bedroom. It was commonly used across many cultures before the introduction of indoor plumbing and flushing toilets.

The term "chamber" is an older word for bedroom. Chamber pots are also known by several other names, including Jordan, jerry, guzunder, po (possibly derived from the French term "pot de chambre"), potty pot, potty, thunder pot, or thunder mug. They may also be referred to as chamber utensils or bedroom ware.

Chamber pots were utilized in ancient Greece, at least since the 6th century BC. The adoption of indoor flush toilets began to replace chamber pots in the 19th century, although they remained common until the mid-20th century. The alternative to using a chamber pot was to visit an outhouse.

This earthenware pot is inscribed with a poem called 'Marriage':

This Pot is A Present Sent
Some mirth to make is only meant
We hope the same you'll not refuse,
But keep it safe and of it Use
When you want to Piss
Remember them who sent you this present
and the additional lines
What do I see,
Keep me clean and use me well
and what I see I shall not tell.

Chamber Pot, (cont.)

In China, chamber pots were prevalent. One notable example is a wealthy salt merchant from Yangzhou, who extravagantly commissioned a gold chamber pot so tall that he needed a ladder to reach it. Today, chamber pots are still in use in areas without indoor plumbing.

In the Philippines, they are commonly referred to as arinola. Philippine mythology suggests that giving newlyweds a chamber pot will ensure them prosperity.

Chamber pots could be disguised as chairs (known as a close stool) or stored in cabinets to hide them. This type of nightstand is called a commode, which later also became synonymous with "toilet." In homes without such furniture, chamber pots were often kept under the bed.

Modern commode toilets and bedpans, used by bedbound or disabled individuals, are variants of the chamber pot.

A related item is the bourdalou or bourdaloue, a small, handheld, oblong ceramic pot used in 17th- and 18th-century France. This device allowed women to urinate conveniently while standing or crouching, reducing the risk of soiling their clothing, particularly since women at the time did not typically wear two-legged underwear.

Gardyloo

Edinburgh, Scotland in the first half of 1700s was an overcrowded, unsanitary place. More than 50,000 people were crammed within the city walls, livestock wandered freely down the streets and a holler of "gardyloo" gave passersby the message to move away - sharpish.

Coming from the French expression, "Prenez garde a l'eau!" - meaning literally 'beware of the water' - gardyloo was the phrase shouted from the upper floors of tenement buildings by residents as they emptied their chamber pots from the windows above.

People knew to watch out when they heard the phrase "Gardyloo" hollered from above. Tenements in Scotland's capital during the 18th century could be as tall as 14 stories high and had no electricity, running water and or lavatories (inside or out). Toilets at that time were simply a bucket filled up during the day and it was the job - usually of the women and children - to empty them out.

People living on the bottom floor of dwellings could walk outside and empty the contents onto the close, but for those ten, eleven, twelve floors up, opening the window and emptying chamber pots was a common occurrence.

In 1749, the 'Nastiness Act' was passed, which decreed waste could only be tossed out between 10 pm, when the bells struck at the St.Giles High Kirk, and 7am the next morning. Legend has it that the 12th century French King Phillipe Auguste was covered in the contents of a chamber pot, and decreed that all upstairs residents were obliged to warn pedestrians before throwing out waste water.

Proper sewage systems in Edinburgh meant that by the 1930s the term became obsolete, but the word is far from forgotten. In fact, the Nastiness Act to this day has never been repealed, so technically throwing your waste out of the window is still legal - but passersby these days may be a little less forgiving.

John

John" is a slang term for a bathroom, especially in the United States and Canada. Many believe it to cynically be named for Sir John Harrington, inventor of Britain's first flushing toilet in the 16th and 17th centuries. It may also come from the medieval names "Jake" and "Jack", which were used to describe small, smelly restrooms.

The term is thought to have been popularized due to Harrington, one of the 102 god-children of Queen Elizabeth I. He became prominent in her court, and was known as her "saucy Godson." His poetry and other writings caused him to fall in and out of favor with her. Elizabeth encouraged his writing, but his work was often marked by gross robust humor, extravagance of caricature, and a risqué naturalisms.

Harington also described England's first flushing toilet he called the Ajax, a bastardization of the name "jakes", then a slang word for toilet. It was installed at his manor in Kelston. This forerunner to the modern flush toilet had a flush valve to let water out of the tank, and a wash-down design to empty the bowl. What it lacked was an S-bend or U-bend to curb noxious smells, which was later invented by Alexander Cumming.

Although Harrington wasn't by any means the first to invent a flushing toilet (there are references to flushing toilets going all the way back to around 2600 BC), his invention was an innovation in Britain at the time and it was commonly thought that he was the inventor.

I've changed my toilets name from John to Jim. It sounds pretty good when I say I've been to the Jim twice today.

Monkey Closets

Of all the technological marvels and innovative designs showcased at The Great Exhibition of 1851, there is one invention that we still use frequently today without fully appreciating its brilliance. For many, it has been a lifesaver—especially after a lunchtime drink.

At the Exhibition, a Brighton plumber named George Jennings installed his so-called "Monkey Closets" in the Retiring Rooms of The Crystal Palace. These "Monkey Closets" created a buzz as they were the first public toilets anyone had ever encountered. During the Exhibition, 827,280 visitors paid a penny each to use them. For that penny, they received a clean seat, a towel, a comb, and even a shoe shine.

When the Exhibition ended and The Crystal Palace was relocated to Sydenham, there were plans to close the toilets. However, Jennings convinced the organizers to keep them open. They agreed, and the penny toilets went on to generate approximately $1,300 (over 50,000 in todays dollars) in revenue each year.

Following the success of Jennings' lavatories at The Crystal Palace, public toilets began to appear on the streets. A few years later, one was introduced specifically for women. These "Public Waiting Rooms" featured water closets set within wooden enclosures.

Public toilets gained popularity after Mr. Thomas Crapper made improvements to Jennings' original flushing mechanism, which guaranteed "a certain flush with every pull."

Print by George Cruickshank, illustrating the poem "Royal Address of Cadwallader - Water-King of Southwark"; a satire on water pollution of the river Thames, c. 1832

The 'Great Stink' of 1858

For centuries the River Thames had been used as a dumping ground for the capital's waste and as the population grew, so did the problem.

The 'Great Stink' of 1858 was a significant event in Central London during July and August of that year, when the smell of untreated human waste and industrial effluent along the banks of the River Thames became so unbearable that Parliament had to close. The hot weather exacerbated the situation, which had been worsening for years due to an aging and inadequate sewer system that emptied directly into the Thames.

Authorities believed that the miasma from the effluent was responsible for transmitting contagious diseases, and three outbreaks of cholera prior to the Great Stink were attributed to the ongoing issues with the river. The overwhelming odor and fears about its health risks prompted action from both national and local authorities who had been contemplating solutions to the problem. They accepted a proposal from civil engineer Joseph Bazalgette to redirect the effluent eastward through a network of interconnecting sewers that sloped toward outfalls located beyond the metropolitan area.

Bazalgette's work effectively ended the dumping of sewage onto the shores of the Thames and contributed to halting cholera outbreaks; his efforts are believed to have saved more lives than those of any other Victorian official. His sewer system continues to operate into the 21st century, servicing a city with a population of over eight million.

Brick sewers had been constructed in London since the 17th century when sections of the Fleet and Walbrook rivers were covered for this purpose. In the century leading up to 1856, over a hundred new sewers were built in London, resulting in around 200,000 cesspits and 360 sewers by that time. Some cesspits leaked methane and other gases, which could sometimes catch fire and explode, while many existing sewers were in

A 19th century woman drops her tea-cup in horror upon viewing a magnified drop of polluted Thames water, which was a prime source of water-borne diseases such as cholera and typhoid.

The 'Great Stink' of 1858, (cont.)

disrepair. Throughout the early 19th century, efforts were made to improve the water supply for Londoners.

By 1858, many medieval wooden water pipes were being replaced with iron ones. The introduction of flushing toilets and a significant increase in the city's population—from just under one million to three million—led to more water being flushed into the sewers, along with the associated waste. Outflows from factories, slaughterhouses, and other industrial activities further strained the already failing sewer system.

Much of this effluent either overflowed or discharged directly into the Thames. The smell was very bad and common to the whole of the water; it was the same as that which now comes up from the gully-holes in the streets; the whole river was, for the time, a real sewer." The stench from the river became so overwhelming that in 1857, the government poured chalk lime, chloride of lime, and carbolic acid into the Thames to mitigate the odor.

During the Victorian era, the prevailing theory regarding the transmission of contagious diseases was the miasma theory. This theory held that most communicable diseases were caused by inhaling contaminated air, which could come from rotten corpses, sewage, decaying vegetation, or even the breath of sick individuals.

Miasma (stink) was widely believed to be the vector for cholera transmission, a disease that was feared due to its rapid spread and high fatality rates. London's first major cholera
epidemic occurred in 1831, claiming 6,536 lives. This was followed by a second outbreak in 1848–49, which resulted in 14,137 deaths in the city, and a further outbreak in 1853–54 that took an additional 10,738 lives.

During the second outbreak, John Snow, a London-based physician, observed that death rates were higher in areas served by the Lambeth and Southwark and Vauxhall water companies. In 1849, he published a paper titled "On the Mode of Communication of Cholera," proposing the theory of water-borne transmission.

Outhouse

An outhouse, known by various names such as bog, dunny, long-drop, netty, or privy, is a small structure separate from a main building that covers a toilet. This toilet is typically either a pit latrine or a bucket toilet, though other forms of dry (non-flushing) toilets may exist. The term "outhouse" can also refer to the toilet itself, not just the structure.

Outhouses were used in urban areas of developed countries well into the second half of the twentieth century and are still common in rural areas and cities of developing nations.

These structures vary in design and construction. By definition, outhouses are outside the dwelling and are not connected to plumbing, sewer, or septic systems. The World Health Organization recommends that they be constructed a reasonable distance from the house to balance easy access with odor concerns.

The primary purpose of an outhouse is to provide privacy and comfort for the user; its walls and roof offer a visual shield and some protection from the elements. Additionally, the outhouse helps prevent rainwater from flooding the toilet hole, which could wash untreated waste into the surrounding soil before it has the chance to decompose.

Outhouses are typically simple and utilitarian, constructed from lumber or plywood, so they can be easily moved when the pit fills up. Depending on the size of the pit and frequency of use, this relocation can occur fairly often, sometimes even yearly.

Once a house's pit got full, it'd be topped off with dirt and forgotten as the grass overtook it, and the outhouse itself would be moved over another hole

Outhouse, (cont.)

somewhere else in the yard. Some pits lasted five or 10 years; others not so long, based on how quickly they filled up and how deep they were dug.

The floor plans of outhouses usually take rectangular or square shapes, though hexagonal designs have also been made. The arrangements inside the outhouse differ by culture. In Western societies, many have at least one seat with a hole, positioned above a small pit. In contrast, some older outhouses in rural areas of European countries feature a hole with two indents for the user's feet.

In Eastern societies, a hole in the floor is common, with users crouching above it. A roll of toilet paper is often available, although old corn cobs, leaves, or other types of paper may be used instead.

There is no standard decoration for outhouse doors. The widely recognized crescent moon symbol on American outhouses was popularized by cartoonists and has an unclear historical basis. Some authors suggest this practice began during the colonial period as a way to designate "men" and "ladies" for an illiterate population, using the sun and moon as symbols for the sexes. Others dismiss this theory as an urban legend. What is clear is that the purpose of the hole is for ventilation and light, and there were a wide variety of shapes and placements used.

"Outhouse tipping" was the act of intentionally overturning an outhouse, once a popular Halloween prank.

Opposite: A two-story outhouse in Michigan. What could possibly be worse than living on the first floor?

Toilet

Throughout history, humans have commonly practiced open defecation or used latrines and outhouses, particularly in rural areas. In cities, chamber pots were widely used, with their contents often discarded into streets or drains. However, some ancient civilizations had more advanced sanitation systems. The Indus Valley civilization, for example, featured private flush toilets, while the Greeks and Romans used public toilets, sometimes connected to early sewer systems.

During the medieval period, monastic latrines, known as reredorters, were occasionally integrated into sophisticated water systems that helped dispose of waste without contaminating drinking, cooking, or washing water. In the early modern era, municipal outhouses contributed to "night soil" collection, an important source of nitrates for gunpowder.

In 1800, Buckingham Palace had no bathroom.

The 19th century saw improvements in outhouse designs, including the privy midden and the pail closet. Indoor toilets were initially a luxury, accessible mainly to the wealthy, and only gradually became available to the lower classes. As late as the 1890s, London's building codes did not require indoor toilets in working-class housing.

In early 20th-century England, some homes had an indoor toilet for the owners while retaining an outhouse for servants. Others featured indoor toilets accessible only from outside. After World War I, new housing developments in London and its suburbs routinely included indoor toilets. Bathrooms, however, took longer to become standard, often appearing in working-class homes around the same time. Due to plumbing considerations, flush toilets

Toilet (cont.)

were typically placed near or within bathrooms, often above the kitchen for convenience.

In upper-class households, early lavatories functioned primarily as washrooms, with sinks installed near bedrooms. Meanwhile, lower-class homes typically relied on collapsible tubs for bathing.

British society historically resisted placing toilets inside bathrooms. In 1904, architect Hermann Muthesius observed that English homes rarely combined the two, as it was considered inappropriate. When cost-saving measures eventually led to integrating toilets into bathrooms, the shift was met with criticism. In 1876, progressive architect Edward William Godwin designed affordable housing that included toilets within bathrooms, a move that sparked controversy.

Today, homes in the U.S. and much of Europe typically feature combined bathrooms and toilets. However, separate toilet rooms remain common in British homes and are still offered as a design option. In countries like France and Japan, separate toilets are preferred for reasons of hygiene and privacy. Modern homes with separate toilets often include a sink, while in Japan, some toilets feature built-in sinks that reuse water from handwashing for the next flush. Additionally, Japanese homes often provide special slippers exclusively for use in the toilet area, distinct from those worn elsewhere.

The average American visits the toilet 2,500 times a year. With a U.S. population of 300 million, that adds up to 750 billion trips annually. Some 7 million cell phones a year are dropped into toilets.

America

The one-of-a-kind 18-carat gold toilet weighing just over 215 pounds and valued at $3.5 million was swiped on Sept. 14, 2019, in predawn hours.

The theft occurred in under five minutes from Blenheim Palace, the sprawling English country mansion where British wartime leader Winston Churchill was born.

The satirical work, titled "America" by Italian conceptual artist Maurizio Cattelan, poked fun at excessive wealth. The piece was previously displayed at The Guggenheim Museum in New York.

The statement toilet was fitted at the Guggenheim in 2016, where 100,000 people queued to use it. It was moved to Blenheim and into a chamber opposite the room where Churchill was born, for Cattelan's first solo UK show in over 20 years. The museum offered the work to U.S. President Donald Trump during his first term in office after he asked to borrow a Van Gogh painting.

The working toilet, which could be used with a three-minute time limit to avoid queues, had only been on show for two days when it was stolen.

The toilet has never been recovered but is believed to have been cut up and sold.

Four men have been charged for the theft.

Crapper

It is often claimed in popular culture that the vulgar slang term for human bodily waste, "crap," originated from Thomas Crapper due to his association with toilets. A common version of this story is that American servicemen stationed in England during World War I saw his name on cisterns and began using it as Army slang, saying things like, "I'm going to the crapper."

However, the word "crap" actually has Middle English origins and predates its association with bodily waste. Its most likely etymological roots combine two older words: the Dutch "krappen" (meaning to pluck off, cut off, or separate) and the Old French "crappe" (which refers to siftings, waste, or rejected matter, derived from medieval Latin "crappa"). In English, the term was initially used to refer to chaff, weeds, or other rubbish. According to the Oxford English Dictionary, its first recorded application to bodily waste appeared in 1846, a decade after Crapper was born, in reference to a "crapping ken" or a privy, where "ken" means house.

Thomas Crapper was an English plumber and businessman who founded Thomas Crapper & Co. in London, a plumbing equipment company. His significance regarding toilets has often been exaggerated, largely due to a fictional biography published in 1969 by New Zealand satirist Wallace Reyburn.

Crapper (cont.)

Crapper held nine patents, three of which were for improvements to water closets, such as the floating ballcock. He enhanced the S-bend plumbing trap in 1880 by inventing the U-bend. His company's lavatorial equipment was manufactured on Marlborough Road (now Draycott Avenue), and the company owned the world's first showroom for baths, toilets, and sinks located on King's Road. Crapper was recognized for the quality of his products and received several royal warrants.

Crapper's advertisements often suggested that the siphonic flush was his invention. One such advertisement claimed, "Crapper's Valveless Water Waste Preventer (Patent #4,990) - One movable part only," although patent 4,990 for this minor improvement to the water waste preventer actually belonged to Albert Giblin in 1898. However, Crapper's nephew, George, did improve the siphon mechanism that starts the water flow, and a patent for this development was awarded in 1897.

Manhole covers with Crapper's company's name on them in Westminster Abbey have become one of London's minor tourist attractions.

Head

A "head" is a maritime term used to refer to a ship's bathroom or toilet. This term originated because the toilet was typically located at the front of the ship, near the bowsprit. The term has been in use by the navy since at least 1708.

The name comes from the fact that the wind usually blows from behind the ship, so sailors would go to the "head" to avoid relieving themselves into the wind. These toilets were often simply holes cut into the decking. The positioning of the head was practical because the wind would help carry away odors.

On sailing ships, the toilet was located in the bow, somewhat above the waterline, with vents or slots cut near the floor level. This design allowed regular wave action to wash out the facility. Only the captain had a private toilet near his quarters, which was positioned at the stern of the ship in the quarter gallery.

Plans from 18th-century naval ships do not show the construction of toilet facilities when the ships were first built. The journal of Aaron Thomas aboard HMS Lapwing in the Caribbean Sea during the 1790s mentions that a canvas tube was attached, presumably by the ship's sailmaker, to a superstructure beside the bowsprit near the figurehead. This tube ended just above the normal waterline.

In many modern boats, heads resemble seated flush toilets but utilize a system of valves and pumps that bring seawater into the toilet. In smaller boats, the pump is often hand-operated.

The head on the beakhead of the 17th-century warship Vasa. The toilets are the two square box-like structures on either side of the bowsprit. On the starboard side, there are still minor remnants of the original seat.

Head, (cont.)

After flushing, the waste typically travels to a boat's holding tank. While there are various options for onboard waste management—including chemical toilets, composting heads, and full onboard treatment systems—most boats have a simple marine head connected to a holding tank.

Submarine heads face the challenge of higher water pressure, which makes it more difficult to pump waste out through the hull at greater depths. As a result, early systems were complicated; for instance, the head fitted to the United States Navy's S-class submarine was so intricate that it was described as almost requiring an engineer to operate. Making a mistake could result in waste or seawater being forcibly expelled back into the submarine's hull, leading to incidents such as the loss of the German submarine U-1206.

The toilet on the World War I British E-class submarine was considered so inadequate by the captain of HMS E35 that he preferred the crew to wait until the submarine surfaced at night to relieve themselves. Consequently, many submarines only used the heads as extra storage space for provisions.

Aboard sailing ships during an era when the crew was exclusively male, the heads were primarily used for defecation. For routine urination, however, a "piss-dale" was easier to access and simpler to use. A piss-dale is a lead basin or trough fitted to the inner sides of the bulwarks on sailing ships, serving as a urinal for the crew. This innovation emerged in the 17th century; prior to this, crew members typically used buckets or, more frequently, urinated over the rails of the ship. This practice posed a risk of falling overboard and drowning, as few sailors could swim. The piss-dale was akin to a "seat of ease," a euphemism for a sitting toilet located in the beakhead.

Toilet on USS Growler, a Regulus II guided missile submarine

Squat Toilets

An Asian Squat toilet, like its name, is used for squatting rather than sitting. This means that the posture for defecation and female urination is to place one foot on each side of the toilet drain or hole and to squat over it.

Squat toilets are used worldwide but are particularly common in Asian and African nations and some Muslim countries. In many of those countries, anal cleansing with water is also the cultural norm and easier to perform than with toilets used in a sitting position.

Some handy tips for squat toilet newbies:

• Empty your pants pockets before squatting—gravity isn't your friend here.

• Don't drop your pants all the way down. Leave them above your knees so they don't interfere with the critical thoroughfare when you assume the position.

• The hole in the toilet? That's your target. Aim to position yourself directly above it for a clean drop.

• Don't bring reading material. If you squat too long, your legs may go numb.

Squat toilet fans claim the squatting defecation posture is more physiological, ideal, and relaxed.

Royal Flush

While sitting on the throne in the small reading room, here is something to ponder. Few things in our daily lives have as many names or nicknames as the humble toilet. Drawn from languages of every continent, cultural vernacular and historical derivations, the list is a testament to Mr. Crapper's legacy.

- Banheiro
- Banjoja
- Bañu
- Bean-Jacks
- Biffy
- Bog
- Bowl
- Can
- Cesso
- Chamber Pot
- Chiottes
- Choo
- Cloakroom
- Coalfabias
- Comfort Room
- Comfort Station
- Commode
- Convenience
- Cloakroom
- CR
- Crapper
- Crane
- Dunny
- Dunnekin
- El Baño
- Facilities
- Forakers
- Gabinetto
- Garderobe
- Head
- Hopper
- House of Ease
- Huuschen
- Il Bagno
- Jakes
- Jax
- Jericho
- Jerry
- John
- Johnny House
- Karsy
- Kamot
- Khazi
- Latrine
- Lav
- Lavatory
- Little Boys/Girls Room
- Loo
- Long Drop
- Necessarium
- Necessary
- Netty
- Outhouse
- Oval Office
- Pan
- Porcelain God
- Po
- Pool
- Pot
- Potty
- Powder room
- Privy
- Reading Room
- Restroom
- El Retrete
- Sanitarios
- Seat
- Los Servicios
- Shit shack
- Small house
- Stool
- Sukhā
- Swanie
- Thunder Mug
- Thunder Box
- Tinkletorium
- Toilet
- Toilette
- Smallest Room
- Throne
- Throne Room
- Toire
- The Vin
- W.C.
- Wash room
- Water Closet

Kybo

When nature calls and there's no restroom in sight, knowing how to properly handle the situation is a valuable skill.

It's an essential outdoor skill because, as the Boy Scout Handbook wisely states, "getting rid of human waste outdoors requires special care." The third principle of the Leave No Trace guidelines emphasizes the importance of properly disposing of waste.

The process starts with digging a cathole or latrine:
- Choose a location at least 200 feet (about 75 steps) away from water sources, campsites, and trails.
- Dig a hole 6 to 8 inches deep using your heel, a stick, or a trowel.
- "Follow nature's flow."
- Cover the hole with soil after use.
- Restore the ground by replacing leaves, pine needles, or other natural cover.
- Insert a stick into the ground as a marker to prevent others from digging in the same spot.
- Sanitize your hands with hand sanitizer or wash with soapy water.

Nature takes care of the rest. Microorganisms in the topsoil will naturally break down the waste. If you use biodegradable toilet paper, it will also decompose over time.

Tiger Toilet

Sanitation is a distressing problem in India, especially in the rural regions. The biggest setback related to sanitation is the lack of access to adequate sanitation facilities, particularly in rural and peri-urban areas where open defecation is widespread and access to sewage systems is restricted. 750 million people, or 60% of the country's total population, do not have access to adequate sanitation facilities. Each year, 300,000 people die from diarrhea and related diseases.

Poor sanitation makes a significant contribution to this disease burden. Children under the age of five are the worst affected. Repeated diarrheal episodes also lead to malnutrition, and India is home to millions of chronically malnourished children.

Without access to proper sanitation facilities, women and girls face a loss of privacy and dignity and are also exposed to serious risks of sexual and physical violence.

Tiger Worm Toilets (sometimes known as vermifilter toilets) contain composting worms inside the toilet that digest faeces, reducing the accumulation rate and significantly extending the lifetime of the toilet. A worm colony can live inside the toilet indefinitely if the correct environmental conditions are maintained.

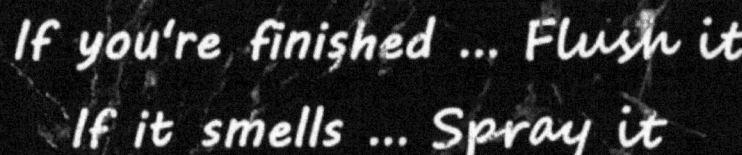

Public Potty Etiquette

Using public restrooms is a routine part of life, yet etiquette often gets overlooked. Following these simple guidelines, you help maintain a clean, respectful, and less weird space for all users.

Be Patient
Discovering what appears to be a full house of closed doors than entering a restroom can be a tinkle emergency nightmare. Most stalls have indicators showing whether they're occupied or available. Gently test the handle; if it doesn't move, step back and wait. Rattling or jiggling a locked stall door is impolite and embarrassing when the occupant eventually emerges. There's no way to hurry people up, so be patient and wait your turn.

Keep Conversations Outside
Restrooms are meant to be quiet spaces. Just because the bathroom acoustics are good is no reason to sing.

Close the Toilet Seat
Always leave the stall as you found it, ensuring a clean and orderly space for the next user. This includes putting the toilet seat down! Pretend your wife is watching.

Personal Space
If possible, leave a gap between you and other users. For example, if the first stall is occupied, choose the third instead of the second.

Keep It in the Bowl
Restroom messes are an unfortunate reality. If you make a mess, take a moment to clean up after yourself. Men, avoid splashing on the floor. Stand closer; it's shorter than you think.

Wash Your Hands
The importance of handwashing cannot be overstated! While it's tempting to rush out, skipping handwashing is unhygienic and creepy.

Don't Linger in the Stall
Long lines can form in busy restrooms, and no one wants to wet their pants because you're doom scrolling through your phone.

Making a Clean Sweep

It's ready to roll when duty calls.
It always gets to the bottom of things
and it all works out in the end.

Thank you for remaining seated through the
entire performance.

The History *of* Toilet Paper

If you've ever found yourself in a small reading room, debating the merits of 2-ply versus 1-ply, consider this: before toilet paper, people relied on an array of materials for hygiene. Leaves, coconuts, sponges, moss, corncobs, newspapers, and magazines all served the purpose at various points in history.

Toilet paper traces its origins to 2nd-century China, where it was first crafted from raw silk. In Russia, paper production began in the 17th century under the reign of Alexei Mikhailovich, but it wasn't until the 19th century—when the paper industry boomed—that toilet paper gained widespread sanitary use.

The choice of wiping materials often depended on local resources. Coastal communities used mussel shells, while Hawaiians turned to coconut husks. The wealthy enjoyed more luxurious options, such as lace or woolen cloth.

In Ancient Rome, people used a communal sponge on a stick, rinsed in saltwater or vinegar between uses. Affluent Romans preferred sponges made from fine wool, sometimes soaked in rose water for extra freshness. Meanwhile, Colonial Americans favored cornstalks.

A major shift in hygiene habits came in the 1700s with the rise of daily newspapers. Coincidentally, this was around the time of Gutenberg's printing press. In the 19th century, catalogs like the Farmers' Almanac (established in 1818) and Sears Roebuck (founded in 1893) became popular bathroom staples, thanks to their soft paper and the convenient hole for hanging in outhouses. Even so, corn cobs remained a common alternative for many.

By the 1930s, as magazines began using glossier paper, catalogs lost favor as a wiping material. England led the way in mass-producing toilet paper in 1880,

(The History *of* Toilet Paper, cont.)

though it was initially rough. Americans, preferring a softer touch, saw the introduction of gentler toilet paper in 1907. The rise of indoor plumbing in the 20th century cemented its place as a household necessity.

Toilet paper's evolution included notable milestones: Joseph Gayetty's 1857 invention of the first commercially sold toilet paper—infused with aloe to treat hemorrhoids—marked the beginning of its widespread use. It was named "The Therapeutic Paper." It contained aloe; 500 sheets cost 50 cents.

In 1890, Irvin and Clarence Scott introduced the toilet paper roll, revolutionizing convenience. The 1930s brought splinter-free toilet paper. Ads claimed that more than 65 percent of middle-age men and women suffered from some sort of rectal disease, largely caused by inferior toilet paper.

The 1950s saw the rise of colored varieties, which later declined due to allergic reactions and environmental concerns in the 1970s.

It's unconfirmed that the Pentagon uses some 666 rolls of toilet paper daily. We do know the building houses 23,000 employees, has 284 restrooms, and that Americans average seven sheets per visit. Back of the napkin math says that's a lot of shit.

Today, toilet paper is softer, stronger, and more absorbent than ever. While it's easy to take for granted, the shortages during the early days of the COVID-19 pandemic were a stark reminder of its importance in daily life.

"If you're embarking around the world in a hot-air balloon, don't forget the toilet paper."

-Sir Richard Branson

Corn Cobs

Before the invention of toilet paper, dried corn cobs were a common choice for cleaning, especially in rural areas. They were abundant, relatively soft, and effective. Native Americans and colonial settlers in North America widely used them due to their availability and practicality.

Once the edible kernels were removed, the cob's grooves and indentations made it efficient at trapping residue. Users could rotate the cob for a thorough clean, and its length helped keep hands away from waste. Surprisingly gentle when dried, corn cobs remained a preferred option in some Western states even after toilet paper became available.

A few of the odd things that humans have used to wipe their rears over the years, most not at all comfortable. These include leaves, sticks, grass, hay, shells, and snow.

Ancient Romans and Greeks also used rounded, smoothed ceramic stones called Pessoi to wipe. As you can probably guess, the hard objects weren't kind.

Soft mosses were undoubtedly far more pleasant for ancient bums. The Vikings, Anglo-Saxons, and Scottish are all thought to have widely wiped with the absorbent, pliable plants. Modern survivalists and camping experts commonly recommend moss when toilet paper isn't available, dubbing it "Green Charmin."

Sailors relied on a "tow rag"—a frayed rope left dangling in the water for repeated use.

Analog Amazon

From 1888 to 1993, the Sears catalog was the Amazon website of its time.

Spanning hundreds of pages, the Sears, Roebuck & Co. catalog offered nearly everything via mail order, from everyday necessities like clothing and appliances to more unexpected items like banjos and even live monkeys. At one point, they even sold entire houses.

But the Sears catalog had a use Amazon could never replicate—it doubled as toilet paper in outhouses. Before commercial toilet paper became widespread, people relied on whatever was available, including corn cobs, newspapers, and magazines. The Sears catalog, with its soft, crinkly pages, became a go-to option, especially in a pinch.

A local newspaper from Axtell, Kansas, captured the catalog's dual purpose in an excerpt from September 16, 1937:

"A train load of Sears Roebuck catalogs arrived at the local post office last week. While the bargains therein may not appeal to the public as they did in the past when money was more plentiful, the evident shortage of this fall's corn crop will cause each recipient to accept the big tome with gratitude."

The habit of hanging catalogs in outhouses was so widespread that, in 1919, the Farmer's Almanac started pre-drilling holes in its publications for easy hanging.

Night Soil Man

To all that believe they have a shitty job, here's proof things could be much, much worse.

The Nightman as the name indicates, worked at night and by laws had to do their work after a certain time. They came in after dark and cleaned out night soil, a historical euphemism for human dookie collected from cesspools, privies, pail closets, pit latrines, privy middens, septic tanks, etc.

In the 1840s Henry Mayhew, an English journalist, described the process as involving a team of three or four men with a tub and a cart.

The "holeman" went into the cesspit and filled the tub either by immersing it or with a shovel, then scraped or washed off the outside of the tub.

The "ropeman" would pull the tub out, and the two "tubmen" would carry the tub, suspended on a pole, to the cart. The waste was then taken to the nightman's yard where it was mixed with ashes and rotting vegetables that had been collected, and then it was sold to farmers as manure for their fields or for the production of gunpowder.

Arming a militia used to be a lot more shitty. Poop and guns have a long history together—one we've all but forgotten thanks to a technology developed at the turn of the 20th century that allowed gunpowder to be made from air instead of poop.

Chimney sweeps and rubbish collectors often worked as nightmen.

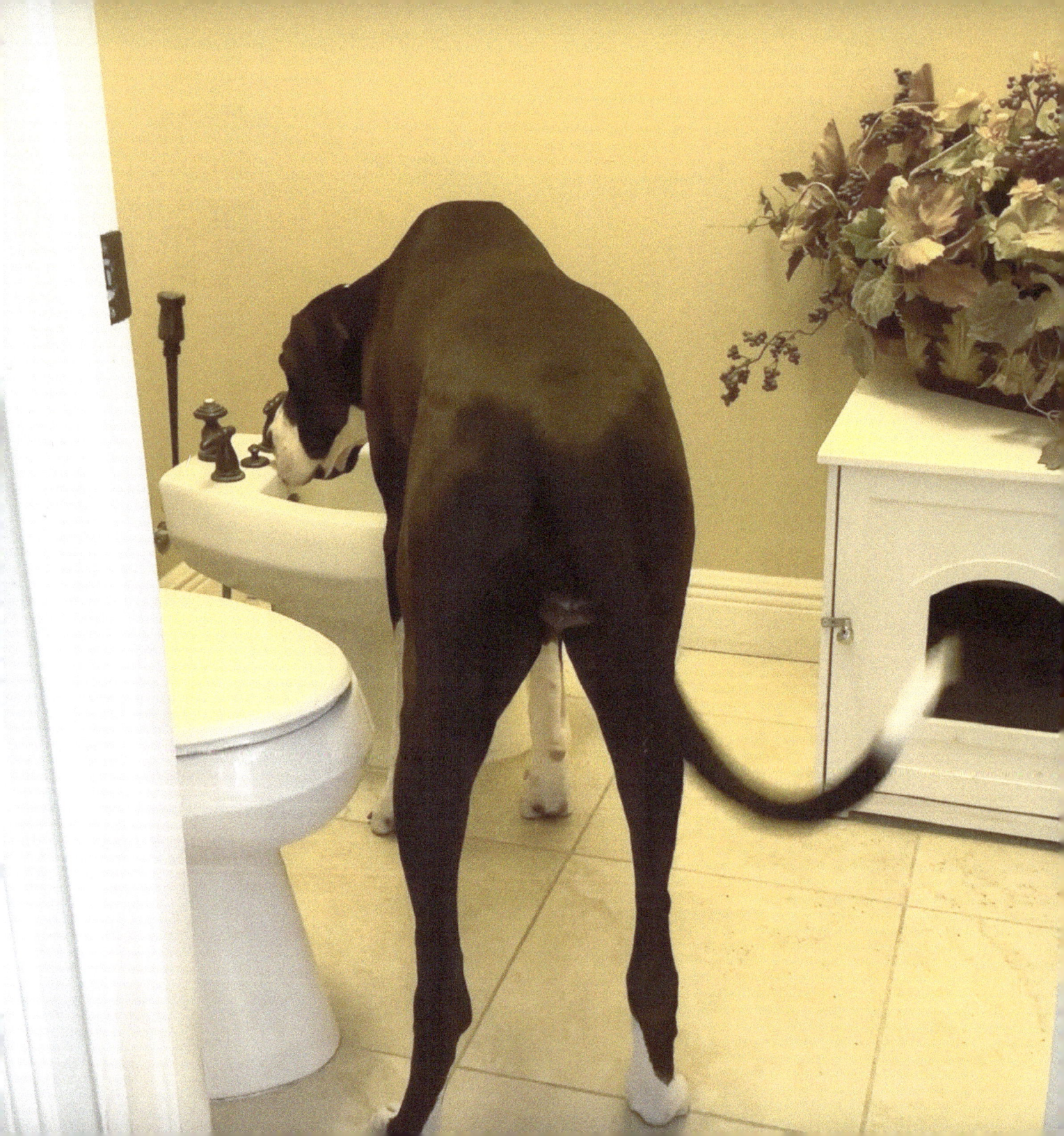

Bum Guns

Long popular in Europe and South America, bidets – devices that use a stream of water to clean up after using the toilet–are becoming more common worldwide.

A famous scene from the 1986 movie Crocodile Dundee captures the confusion many Americans feel when encountering a bidet. Mick Dundee, in his upscale New York City hotel bathroom, struggles to figure out what the contraption is and how to use it. His bewilderment isn't unique–most U.S. bathrooms, even in luxury hotels, lack bidets, making them a novelty for many Americans. By contrast, in parts of Asia, Europe, and South America, a bathroom without a bidet would seem incomplete.

The bidet originated in early 18th-century France, where it got its name from the French word for "horse"– a nod to the way one straddles it. The first known bidet was installed for the French royal family in 1710. Initially placed in bedrooms alongside chamber pots, bidets evolved over time, eventually moving into bathrooms and gaining features like hand pumps for spraying water by 1750.

From its aristocratic French roots, the bidet spread internationally and is now a staple in many countries. It is particularly common in Italy and Portugal, as well as in South America, the Middle East, and East Asia–especially Japan, where around 80 percent of bathrooms include one.

Despite its popularity elsewhere, the bidet never took off in the U.S. During World War II, U.S. soldiers often saw bidets in European brothels, reinforcing the idea that they were linked to immorality. Practicality may have also played a role. American bathrooms are generally smaller, leaving little room for an extra fixture.

In North America alone, an estimated 36.5 billion rolls of toilet paper are used annually, making bidets an eco-friendly alternative. Yet cultural habits die hard - while bidet users see skipping it as unsanitary, those accustomed to toilet paper often find the idea of using water unfamiliar.

False Alarms

Farting is a universal human experience.

It knows no borders; every person from every corner of the globe passes gas. On average, a person farts about 14 times a day. Most importantly, farting is just funny. In a world often clouded by negativity, it's time to lift our spirits by laughing at this natural and humorous phenomenon.

> *"Thar she blows."*
> Herman Melville - Moby Dick

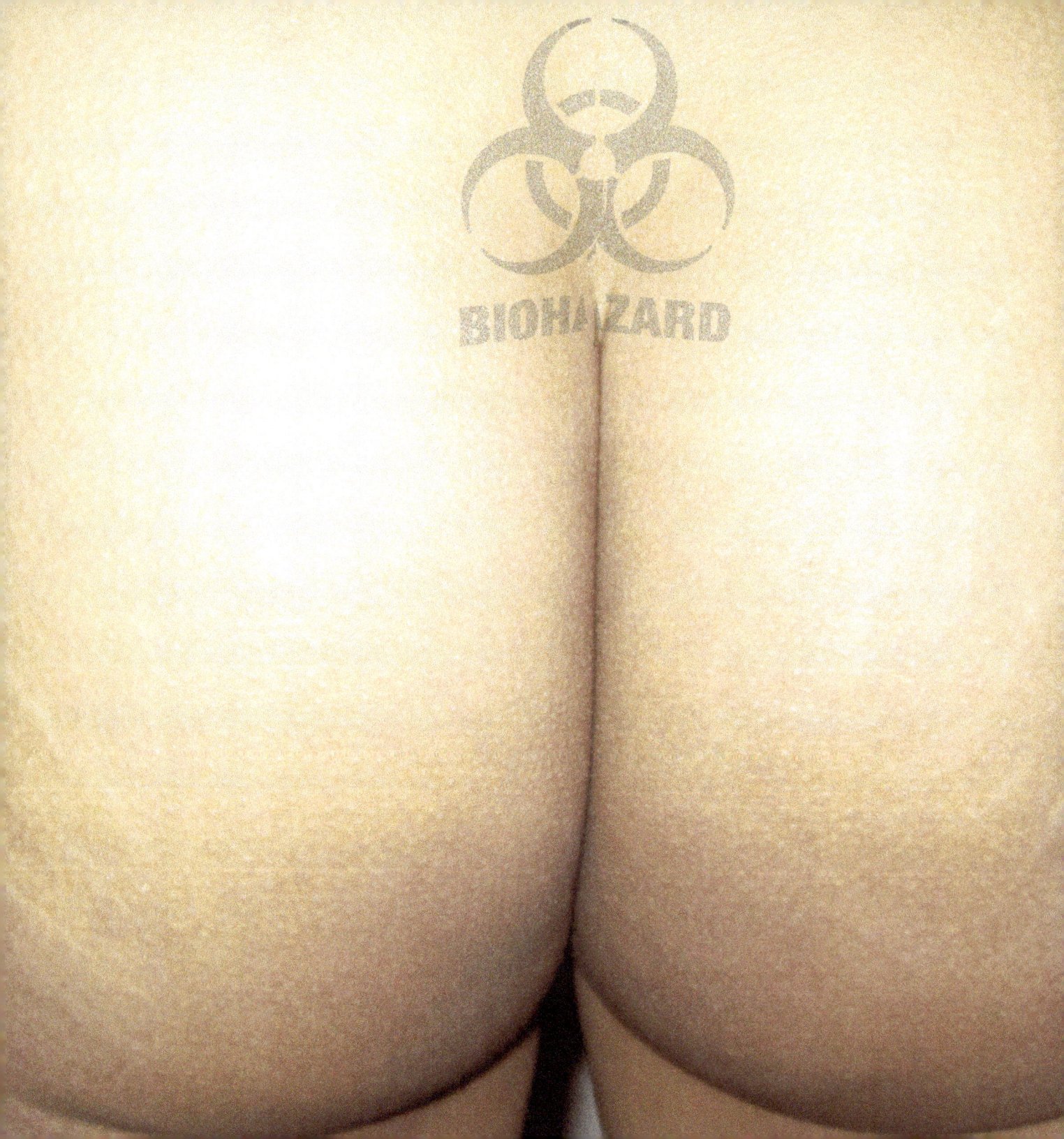

Flatulence

The humble fart slipped into our language long ago, a silent yet undeniable presence. It first appeared as a verb in the 13th century and later took form as a noun by the 15th.

Though I can't imagine anyone actually keeping count, there are reportedly over 300 euphemisms for "flatulence."

It's a universal experience—no one is exempt, and if you have dogs, they're the perpetual scapegoats. Even the world's oldest recorded joke, dating back to 1900 BC, pokes fun at breaking wind. Fast forward to the 21st century, and flatulence remains as hilarious as ever.

In a world rife with cynicism and discord, we should take a moment to celebrate the small things that unite us. Sometimes, those things are acts of kindness and generosity. Other times, they're unexpected contributions from the digestive system.

"Good your grace, an' I had room for such a thundergust within mine ancient bowels, 'tis not in reason I coulde discharge ye same and live to thank God for yt He did choose handmaid so humble whereby to shew his power. Nay, 'tis not I yt have broughte forth this rich o'ermastering fog, this fragrant gloom, so pray you seeke ye further."

- Mark Twain
Conversation, as it was by the Social Fireside,
in the Time of the Tudors.

(It was first published anonymously in 1880,
and finally acknowledged by the author in 1906)

Fart Proudly

A mention of flatulence might conjure up images of bratty high school boys or lowbrow comics. But one of the most eloquent, and least expected commentators on the subject is Benjamin Franklin.

"A Letter to a Royal Academy" or "Fart Proudly" is the name of an essay about flatulence written by Benjamin Franklin c. 1781 while he was living abroad as United States Ambassador to France. It is a prime example of flatulence humor.

"A Letter to a Royal Academy" was composed in response to a call for scientific papers from the Royal Academy of Brussels. Franklin believed that the various academic societies in Europe were increasingly pretentious and concerned with the impractical. Revealing his "bawdy, scurrilous side," Franklin responded with an essay suggesting that research and practical reasoning be undertaken into methods of improving the odor of human flatulence.

Franklin never submitted the essay to the Brussels Academy, but enclosed it in a letter of 16 September 1783 to British philosopher and clergyman Richard Price with whom Franklin had an ongoing correspondences.

"He that lives upon Hope, dies farting."
-Benjamin Franklin, Poor Richard, 1736

(Fart Proudly, cont.)

Franklin's essay begins:

I have perused your late mathematical Prize Question, proposed in lieu of one in Natural Philosophy, for the ensuing year. Permit me then humbly to propose one of that sort for your consideration, and through you, if you approve it, for the serious Enquiry of learned Physicians, Chemists, &c. of this enlightened Age. It is universally well known, that in digesting our common food, there is created or produced in the bowels of human creatures, a great quantity of wind. That the permitting this air to escape and mix with the atmosphere, is usually offensive to the company, from the fetid smell that accompanies it. That all well-bred people therefore, to avoid giving such offense, forcibly restrain the efforts of nature to discharge that wind.

The essay goes on to discuss the way different foods affect the odor of flatulence and to propose scientific testing of farting. Franklin also suggests that scientists work to develop a drug, "wholesome and not disagreeable", which can be mixed with "common Food or Sauces" with the effect of rendering flatulence "not only inoffensive, but agreeable as Perfumes". The essay ends with a pun saying that compared to the practical applications of this discussion, other sciences are "scarcely worth a fart-hing."

Copies of the essay were privately printed by Franklin at his printing press in Passy. After Franklin's death, the essay was long excluded from published collections of Franklin's writing. In the 1960s, it was included in volume 32 of the American Philosophical Society's Papers of Benjamin Franklin.

Since 1929, the essay has sometimes been printed alongside a note from "the publisher to the reader," which claims that the original letter "has been owned by the United States nation since 1881," before going on to further flatulence-related puns: "Dark hints by Franklin's biographers have tainted the air behind its back, but the maiden modesty of even the most contemporary of them has blushed and halted on the brink of its release."

Fizzle/Silent but deadly

While today fizzle has such noble meanings as "to fail or end feebly especially after a promising start," the word has origins of a baser sort. Fizzle is thought to be an alteration of the Middle English fist ("flatus"), which in addition to providing us with the verb for breaking wind quietly, was also munificent enough to serve as the basis for a now-obsolete noun meaning "a silent fart" (feist).

> *Had the Rump but once fizled 'twas the strongest side,*
> *But a Fart has so routed his Troop in their pride,*
> *Though infallible Butler was his guide,*
> *That they are both blown down the wind.*
>
> - Anon.
> A Display of the Headpiece and Codpiece Valour
> of the Most Renowned Colonel Robert Jermy, 1660

The word "feist" has an interesting etymology, originating from Middle English and Proto-Germanic roots, and originally meant "fart", "stink" and also implies "farty dog."

The 1811 slang dictionary defines "fice" (a variant of "feist") as "a small windy escape backwards, more obvious to the nose than ears".

Pumpernickel

At first glance there is no apparent connection between the dark bread, beloved by some, and flatulence. However, looking more closely at the word's etymology ensures that you will have an inappropriate morsel of trivia at many a luncheon to come. Pumpernickel comes from the German words pumpern ("to break wind") and Nickel ("goblin"), apparently due to its indigestibility.

Pumpernickel 'a coarse, dark, slightly sour bread made of unbolted rye', is Germanic. The word was originally used as an insulting term for anyone considered disagreeable. Its elements are pumpern 'to break wind', and Nickel 'a malevolent spirit or demon; devil; rascal', originally a nickname from Nicholas. Pumpernickel, in other words, literally means "farting devil" or "devil's fart"

Presumably the word was applied to the bread in reference to its supposed indigestibility.

Who that drinks Calvert's Butt so clear,
For muddy Mum wou'd stickle?
Or to our English Beef prefer
Sour Grout and Pumpernickle?

- Beef and Butt Beer
A Drinking Song, 1743

Nuns Farts *(Pete De Soeur)*

Nun's farts, is an addictive French Canadian dessert that is made from pie dough; often from left over Tourtière dough, that is layered with butter, brown sugar, then rolled, sliced, placed in a pan, covered with additional brown sugar, and finally baked.

ingredients
- 1 lb favorite pastry dough
- 1/2 cup light brown sugar
- 1 dash cinnamon (optional)
- 3 Tablespoons salted butter
- 2 Tablespoons Milk

Preheat the oven to 350°F.

Roll out pie crust to form a square. Butter pastry with a thin coat of butter. Put a layer of brown sugar over the butter, making sure you cover the entire pie crust.

Roll the pastry to make a long roll (like a cigar), and squeeze the ends tightly so the ingredients don't leak out when cooked. Brush the pastry with milk, making sure the finished edge is on the bottom.

Using a sharp knife cut approximately 1-inch pieces and lay each piece on a parchment covered cookie sheet.

Bake until pastry is golden brown (15 to 18 minutes). Allow them to cool.

These can be frozen for future use for up to a month.

Cut the cheese

Four hundred years after breaking wind for the first time (lexically, at least), English speakers devised another way to avoid cutting to the chase about their ranker emanations with the euphemism "cut the cheese".

In fact, the definition for cut the cheese given in Jonathan E. Lighter's Historical Dictionary of American Slang is "to break wind." Lighter attributes the first-known, pre-print usage of the funky idiom to a "N.Y.C. grade-school student" who boldly asked of their fellows, "Who cut the cheese?", forgetting the tried-and-true maxim that whoever smelt it, dealt it.

Lighter also draws a line back from cut the cheese to 1811's Lexicon Balatronicum: A Dictionary of Buckish Slang, University Wit, and Pickpocket Eloquence, which defined the word cheeser as "a strong smelling fart."

Lactose is a sugar in milk and most dairy products, including cheese and ice cream. People who don't produce enough of the enzyme lactase have difficulty digesting lactose, which is known as lactose intolerance. Increased gas is one symptom of lactose intolerance.

When you think of foods that cause gas, beans are probably at the top. Beans contain a lot of raffinose, a complex sugar the body has trouble digesting. Raffinose passes through the small intestines into the large intestines, where bacteria break it down, producing hydrogen, carbon dioxide, and methane gas.

Like beans, whole grains contain fiber and raffinose, a non-digestable carb. Both are broken down in the large intestine, which may cause gas. Your gas response, however, will vary based on the amount of fiber and non-digestible carbs in whole grain foods as well as your individual tolerance.

Letting Polly Out of Jail

You are attempting to commit a social tautology. If you just farted, there is absolutely no need to tell anybody about it. They will already have worked it out for themselves.

Air biscuit
Air tulip
Anal audio
Anal exhale
Anal salute
Anus applause
Ass acoustics
Ass flapper
Back draft
Back-end blowout
Back blast
Baking brownies
Bark
Barking spider
Barn burner
Beep your horn
Belching clown
Benchwarmer
Blast
Blat
Blurp
Blurt
Bomber
Boom-boom
Booty bomb
Booty cough
Bottom blast
Bottom burp
Break wind
Brown cloud
Brown haze
Brown thunder
Bubbler
Bull snort
Bumsen burner
Bung blast

Burner
Burp out the wrong end
Bust ass
Butt bazooka
Butt bongos
Butt cheek screech
Butt dumpling
Butt sneeze
Butt trumpet
Butt tuba
Butt yodeling
Call of the wild burrito
Cheek squeak
Cheeser
Colon bowlin'
Cornhole clap
Cornhole tremor
Crack concert
Crack splitters
Crap call
Cut one
Cut the cheese
Drifter
Droppin' stink bombs
Duck call
Exhume the dinner corpse
Fanny beep
Fanny frog
Fecal fume
Fire in the hole
Fizzler
Flatus
Floater
Fluffy
Free speech
Frump

Gas
Great brown cloud
Grundle rumble
Gurgler
Heinie hiccup
Hisser
Honker
Horton hears a poo
Hot wind
Hottie
Human hydrogen Bomb
Insane in the methane
Lay an egg
Levi wind tunnel
Mouse on a motorcycle
Nasty cough
O-ring oboe
One-man salute
Orchestra practice
Panty burp
Peter
Pewie
Poof
Poop gopher
Pootsa
Pop tart
Power puff
Puffer
Putt-putt
Quack
Quaker
Raspberry
Rattler
Rectal turbulence
Ripass
Ripper

Roar from the rear
Rump ripper
Rump roar
Silent but deadly
Silly cyanide
Slider
Sphincter siren
Sphincter whistle
Spitter
Split the seam
Squeaker
Stale wind
Steam-press your Calvins
Steamer
Step on a duck
Step on a frog
Stink it up
Stinker
Stinky
Taint tickle
Tear ass
Thunder down under
Thurp
Toot your own horn
Tootsie
Trouser cough
Trouser trumpet
Trunk bunk
Turd tremors
Turtle burp
Tushy tickler
Under thunder
Wallop
Whiff
Whoopee
Whopper

Who wrote this crap?

I first knew I was destined to write this book when I noticed that the chair in my office flushed.

A frequent visitor to the small room, Dr. Maddog, a.k.a. Mark Donnelly, PhD. is an artist, educator, community activist, and a proud husband and father of four amazing adults.

Many believe that the older Dr. Donnelly gets, the younger his imagination becomes. He warmly embraces fourth grade fart jokes.

He is the author of 42 books (and counting), including children's books like: *My Name is Rocky, Theresa's Sock, Where the Bathwater Goes, The Worm Doctor, Brittney is a cat today, Twenty-Five Cents, But I don't want to be a butterfly, For short, A Journey for Peace,* and *Where Did My Wonder Go?*

He has also written about Western New York's history, waterfront, architecture, Buffalo winters, and a series of novelty cookbooks.

As one of the region's premier photographers, Mark's work has appeared in numerous exhibitions and galleries, including the Albright-Knox Art Gallery, The NACC, Burchfield-Penney Art Center, Rodman Hall Arts Centre, and the Art Gallery of Hamilton.

  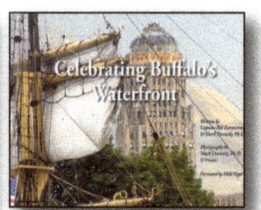  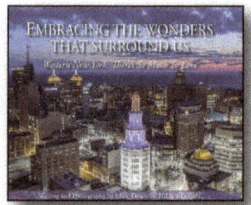

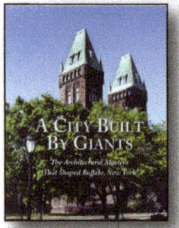    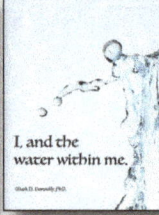  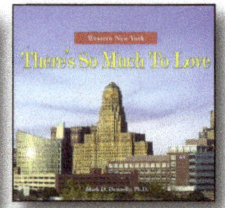

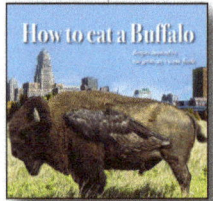     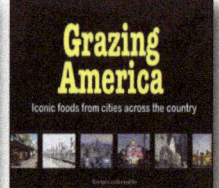

 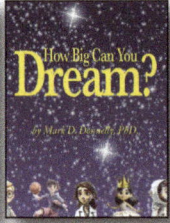   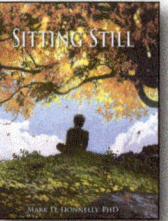 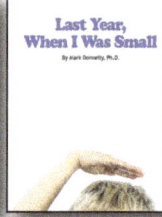 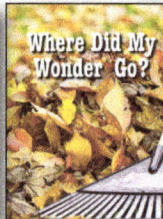 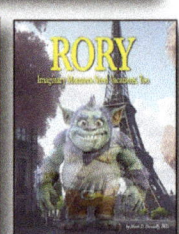

 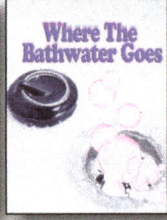  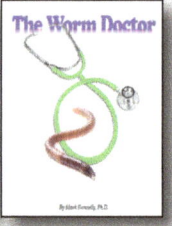    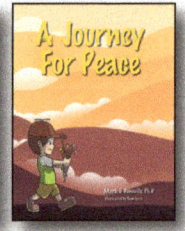

(More of Dr. Donnelly's crappy books.)

   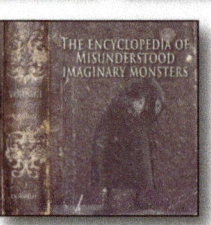

www.ingramcontent.com/pod-product-compliance
Lightning Source LLC
Chambersburg PA
CBHW051551220426
43671CB00025B/2997